Mysterious Encounters

Oak Island Treasure Pit

by Shirley Raye Redmond

KIDHAVEN PRESS
A part of Gale, Cengage Learning

GALE
CENGAGE Learning

Detroit • New York • San Francisco • New Haven, Conn • Waterville, Maine • London

LIBRARY OF CONGRESS CATALOGING-IN-PUBLICATION DATA

Redmond, Shirley-Raye, 1955-
  Oak Island treasure pit / by Shirley Raye Redmond.
    p. cm. -- (Mysterious encounters)
  Includes bibliographical references and index.
  ISBN 978-0-7377-5140-6 (hardcover)
  1. Oak Island Treasure Site (N.S.)--Juvenile literature. 2. Treasure troves--Nova Scotia--Oak Island (Lunenburg)--Juvenile literature. 3. Oak Island (Lunenburg, N.S.)--Antiquities--Juvenile literature. 4. Oak Island (Lunenburg, N.S.)--History--Juvenile literature. I. Title.
  F1039.O35R44 2010
  971.6'23--dc22
<div align="right">2010026400</div>

KidHaven Press
27500 Drake Rd.
Farmington Hills, MI 48331

ISBN-13: 978-0-7377-5140-6
ISBN-10: 0-7377-5140-1

Printed in the United States of America
1 2 3 4 5 6 7 15 14 13 12 11

Printed by Bang Printing, Brainerd, MN, 1ˢᵗ Ptg., 03/2011

Contents

Chapter 1

Buried Treasure

In the Canadian province of Nova Scotia, Oak Island is the most famous and mysterious piece of real estate. It is nestled next to the south coast of Halifax, Nova Scotia's capital city, and is surrounded by the calm blue-green waters of Mahone Bay. The peanut-shaped island is a home to birds, rabbits, and even deer. Most of the island is covered with spruce and fir trees, wild apple trees, and blueberry and raspberry bushes. Another portion of Oak Island is honeycombed with pits, small craters, and boreholes. For more than 200 years, legends of long-lost pirate loot have lured many treasure seekers to the island. Tales of vengeful ghosts have kept others away. In 1763 long-ago residents of Chester, on

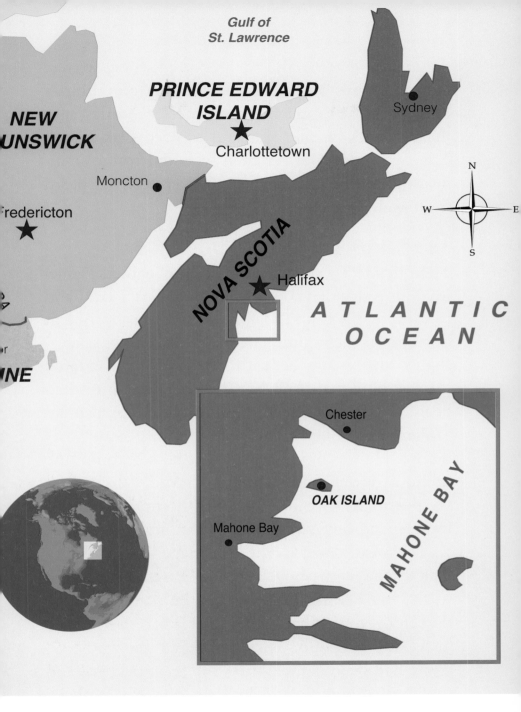

The Canadian province of Nova Scotia is home to the tiny Oak Island.

the mainland across the bay, reported seeing strange lights and fires on Oak Island. Fearing bloodthirsty buccaneers, who sailed these waters centuries ago, the residents on the mainland avoided Oak Island. The two brave Chester men who did row over to investigate one evening were never seen or heard from again.

Teenage Treasure Seekers

Then in 1795 a sixteen-year-old boy named Daniel McGinnis decided to go fishing on Oak Island and to explore. He found a large oak tree in a clearing at one end of the island. There was a shallow, saucer-shaped depression beneath the oak. He wondered if something had been buried there. McGinnis had heard tales about Scottish sailor and pirate Captain William Kidd burying his booty on this island years before. He was now hopeful that he had found the **cache** of jewels and gold coins. Wildly excited by the possibility, McGinnis hurried home and told his friends Anthony Vaughn and John Smith.

The next day the three teenagers returned to Oak Island with shovels and pickaxes. They went to the big oak tree. There was the stub of a large branch overhead that looked as if it had been cut or sawed off long ago. They wondered nervously if a pirate had been hanged from the great oak tree and then buried beneath it. They began to dig. Without realizing it, the boys had launched an eager search for buried treasure that would last for more than

Fueled by rumors of buried pirate treasure, three teenage boys began digging on Oak Island in 1795.

200 years!

After several weeks of hard labor, the boys had dug a hole 10 feet (3.04m) deep and discovered a platform of tightly fitted oak logs. They were puzzled, but excited too. The logs of the platform were rotten. This proved that someone had buried something here many years ago.

After digging to a depth of 30 feet (9.14m), the

Mahone Bay was named after *mahonne*, an old French word for a sailing vessel that was popular with coastal pirates in the Mediterranean.

teens gave up. All they had discovered after their hard work were two more platforms of oak logs, one copper coin dated 1713, a whistle belonging to a **boatswain**, and a seaweed-covered rock in a small bay called Smith's Cove. The rock had a rusty iron ring bolted to it. The ringbolt made the teens believe that pirates had indeed landed on the island and tied their boat here. The strange platforms built into the underground shaft that was 13 feet (4m) in diameter convinced them that something valuable was buried on Oak Island.

Still hopeful, they returned to the mainland. The teens tried to convince their friends and neighbors to help them dig up the buried treasure from what they called the "Money Pit," but the old tales about pirates scared some. Others did not want to work so hard for something they were not really sure they would find at all. The years passed without the boys returning to the island. The pit caved in. McGinnis, Vaughn, and Smith grew up to become farmers, like their fathers before them. They always wondered what lay buried beneath the old oak tree.

Booby Trap!

Then in 1802, Vaughn told a man named Simon Lynds about the legend of the Oak Island Treasure Pit. Lynds was intrigued. He promptly formed the Onslow Company, made up of 30 businessmen willing to finance the purchase of equipment and labor to dig, or **excavate,** the pit. Vaughn, McGinnis, and Smith, now young men in their early twenties, were considered members of the company as well. That summer the excavations reached 90 feet (27.4m). The men became even more puzzled when they hit similar platforms after digging another 10 feet or so. In addition to the well-constructed oak platforms, their digging revealed putty, charcoal, and layers and layers of fibers from coconut husks. Everyone was amazed. Oak Island was more than 1,500 miles (2,414km) north of any coconut trees!

Origin of Coconut Fibers

Botanists have positively identified the coconut fibers on Oak Island. Historians now know that Spaniards often used such fibers as packing material in their ships' cargo holds.

Each time a piece of evidence was unearthed from the pit, it gave treasure hunters hope that something really valuable would be soon be discovered.

Where in the world had the fibers come from? Who had brought them to the island? And why would anyone go to so much trouble?

Members of the Onslow Company continued to excavate until they discovered a large flat stone with strange **inscriptions**, or writing, on it. Eagerly, the men pried the stone from the pit, but no one could make out the odd engravings. Smith, who was now married and living with his family on Oak Island, decided to take the curious stone home with him. The other men kept digging, certain they would soon recover the treasure. But suddenly, they hit a **booby trap.** This hidden trigger caused saltwater to flood the pit. Someone had intended that the treasure of Oak Island should never be retrieved.

The Mysterious Pit

No matter how much water they bailed or how fast they bailed it, the pit remained flooded with seawater. The task was hopeless. In an effort to continue excavating, the men abandoned the first pit and dug a second shaft nearby. This too filled with seawater. The treasure hunters' enthusiasm for digging for long-forgotten riches was dampened. Their money for the project ran out, too. Discouraged, they quit.

Many years passed. McGinnis died, but the tale of his discovery of the mysterious shaft on Oak Island was passed down from one generation to the next. Smith and Vaughan became old men in their 70s, who told their grandchildren stories of when they tried to find pirate treasure. Then in 1849 another group of men formed the Truro Company and raised funds to continue digging for the Oak Island treasure. Smith, Vaughn, and Lynds eagerly showed them the location of the original pit. The new treasure hunters excavated the original shaft in just twelve days, but again, seawater bubbled up into the deep hole and work had to be stopped.

Next time they brought in a drilling engineer armed with a hand-operated **auger,** or drill bit, similar to the kind coal miners use. The engineer screwed his chisel-tipped auger into the earth and removed **cores** of drilled material. At about 98 feet (29.8m), he struck something the men believed to be a wooden container, because the core sample contained splinters of wood. There were also more coconut husk fibers, and best of all, "three small links which had apparently been forced from an **epaulette**. They were gold."[1]

The treasure hunters were thrilled. Here was evidence that something of value was indeed buried in the pit. The problem was that whoever put it there had made sure no one else would be able to recover it without knowing the secret. Again and again, the shaft filled with water. Further digging revealed that the water trap was very complicated and had taken careful engineering. It involved not only the pit, but tunnels, drains, and a filter system. Who had created this amazing booby trap, and why? The discouraged men of the Truro Company did not know. But they were sure of one thing: No one would go to so much trouble if he did not have something very valuable to hide.

Chapter 2

Who Built the Treasure Pit?

Over the years, there have been many theories, or guesses, about what is buried in the Treasure Pit and who put it there. Some say it is the secret stash of knights from long ago. Others believe members of a secret club, such as the Freemasons, built the well-engineered pit to hide a long-lost treasure. Some insist Viking raiders built the pit, or maybe even aliens from outer space. But the most popular theory is that the treasure of Oak Island is pirate booty.

During the 17th century, pirates often attacked the ports and coastlines of Nova Scotia and Newfoundland in Canada. Although the settlers in the small fishing communities did not have much gold and silver to **plunder**, the pirates helped themselves to food and other supplies. They even kidnapped men to work on their ships. The Bahamas-based pirate named Edward Teach, better known as Blackbeard, attacked the eastern coastline of America until 1718. He boasted that he had buried his vast treasure "where none but Satan and myself can find it."[2] Centuries have passed, but no one has found Blackbeard's booty. Could it be buried at the bottom of Oak Island's treasure pit?

Captain Kidd's Pirate Loot

The oldest and most enduring theory is that the Oak Island treasure belonged to Captain William Kidd. Kidd was a famed **privateer** who attacked French and Spanish ships for the King of England. In return for plundering enemy vessels, he and his crew were given a share of all the goods they captured. Over the years, Kidd gathered a great fortune. He even married a wealthy New York widow and lived for a time in New York City.

Then in 1699 Kidd was arrested for murder in Boston, Massachusetts. He was sent back to England and hanged for his crimes on May 23, 1701. The governor of New York received a tip from one of Kidd's companions and rowed to a small island in New York's Long Island Sound. There he discovered one of Kidd's secret treasure troves. The gold, silver, and jewels buried on Gardiner's Island were said to be only a small portion of what Kidd had

This illustration shows Captain Kidd and his crew burying treasure in an unknown location.

Pirate Treasure?

In 1879 farmer William Moser of Lunenberg, only 10 miles (16km) from Oak Island, discovered 200 gold and silver French and Spanish coins—probably pirate treasure—buried on his property.

collected during his days of privateering.

According to one often-told tale, an old sailor died in New England in the mid-1700s. On his deathbed, he had insisted that he had once been a member of Kidd's crew and that he had helped the captain bury an immense fortune on an island east of Boston. The story traveled far and wide and Daniel McGinnis, Anthony Vaughn, and John Smith probably would have heard this story, too. Although the notion that Captain Kidd's treasure is buried in the Treasure Pit is still popular today, skeptics, or doubters, point out that Kidd and his men would not have had the engineering skills to build such a complicated hiding place. Others point out that the copper coin McGinnis discovered on Oak Island was dated 1713—several years after Kidd was hanged in England. If Kidd's missing treasure *is* buried on Oak Island, he did not put it there.

The Crown Jewels of France

One odd theory suggests that the mystery pit contains the French queen Marie Antoinette's crown jewels that went missing in 1791. It is a fact that she and her husband, King Louis XVI, tried to flee France to escape the rebels who wanted to overthrow the French king. They were caught and forced to turn the crown jewels over to the new government. According to one story, the frightened queen secretly gave some of the jewelry to a faithful lady-in-waiting to hold onto and she may have smuggled them out of France. The king and queen were later beheaded. The Royal Treasury was robbed in 1792 when rioters stormed the gates and the seized jewels were stolen.

Over the years many of the crown jewels were returned to the French treasury, but not all. Some

The pearls in this necklace were once owned by French queen Marie Antoinette, whose crown jewels were stolen in 1791. While most of the jewelry was recovered, it is thought that the still-missing pieces might be buried in the Treasure Pit on Oak Island.

have not been found, including two spectacular diamonds worth hundreds of thousands of dollars. No one knows what happened to them. Some suggest that the jewels were smuggled to the Fortress of Louisbourg, north of Oak Island in Cape Breton, Canada, for safekeeping. They point out that the fortress was built in 1713—the same year on the copper coin discovered by young McGinnis decades later. The fortress was a French stronghold for more than 140 years as the French and British battled for military rule in the New World. As many as 6,000 French soldiers and sailors, twelve ships, and nearly 800 guns were once stationed at the Fortress of Louisbourg. French gold was shipped there to use for army payroll and other military expenses.

Over the years the British frequently attacked the fortress. Some think a French officer may have decided to protect the payroll by moving it to Oak Island. Using professional military engineers and the labor of hundreds of soldiers, he could have ordered the construction of the Treasure Pit to hide the gold from the British. It could have served as a secret safe deposit vault during the war years. Later, a different French officer from the Fortress of Louisbourg could have hidden Marie Antoinette's jewels in the secret cache for safekeeping. Some researchers even believe they may have located historical traces of a French woman in the Fortress of

Louisbourg who might have been this same lady-in-waiting. Nothing has been confirmed.

The Mayan Connection

A rather new idea is that Mayan or Aztec laborers from Central America constructed the Treasure Pit. It has been suggested that the Maya fled Mexico in an effort to protect their national treasures from the plundering Spanish. Perhaps they were taken captive by Spanish conquerors. Sailing north along the eastern coastline of America, they may have landed at Oak

This limestone well in Chichen Itza, Mexico, was built by the ancient Mayans. Elements of the Mayan construction style are found in the Treasure Pit on Oak Island, leading some to theorize that Mayan laborers may have constructed the pit.

Island and spent years constructing the secure pit for their gold. At first, this may seem like a farfetched theory. However, in 1961 a man named Eric Hamblin, who enjoyed history and was a scuba diver, spent considerable time off the coast of Oak Island searching for a seabed entrance to the mystery pit. He noticed the watertight chambers called **cofferdams** on the island and made several interesting observations that support the Mayan theory.

For one thing, the Maya used 10 feet (3.048m) as a standard of measurement. The oak platforms in the pit are located at 10-foot intervals or sections. For another, the Maya used limestone for tunneling and as building materials. There is scientific evidence in Mexico to support this. It also explains the layers of ash and charcoal found in the pit—by-products left over after building their watertight chambers. After examining the cofferdams, Ham-

Chain of Gold

According to reports, the town square in the Incan city of Cuzco, Peru, was surrounded by a 300-foot (91.4m) chain of gold. It disappeared before Francisco Pizarro could ship it to Spain.

blin concluded that "the complexity and permanence of the workings are similar to the strength, thoroughness and details of construction of the drains and buildings uncovered among Mayan and Aztec Ruins in Mexico."[3]

Those familiar with the history of the Spanish in the New World say Aztec or Mayan treasure would be worth finding. The Spanish conquistador, or explorer, Hernán Cortés became a fabulously wealthy man after conquering emperor Montezuma and the Aztecs in Mexico in 1521. His share of the plunder was astonishing, even after sending the required one-fifth back to the king in Spain. In 1533 another Spanish explorer, Francisco Pizarro, stripped 700 sheets of pure gold from the walls of a single Incan temple in South America. After looting the empire for eight months, he had seized 24 tons (21.7 metric tons) of gold worth millions of dollars today. Stories continue to be told of some Incan and Aztec noblemen who escaped their Spanish conquerors and took huge amounts of royal treasure with them for safekeeping. But no one knows where they went or what happened to the gold.

Chapter 3

Disappointments and Disaster

By the year 1900 there was still little evidence that any treasure was buried in the booby-trapped pit. The biggest find had been the mysteriously inscribed stone that John Smith had taken home with him decades before. But in 1804 none of the members of the Oak Island Treasure Company considered how important that stone might be in helping them succeed in their search. Over the years, the strange 175-pound (79.37kg) stone with the coded message inscribed on it intrigued many. Several people, including historians and language experts, tried to break the code. One man translated it to mean "forty feet [12.19m] below two million pounds are buried."[4] No one knows if he translated it correctly. The stone disappeared before World War II and there are no photographs of it. Although the strange symbols, or **glyphs,** etched onto the stone have been copied down and examined, modern code breakers have not been able to confirm the translation. Nor can they be sure the glyphs were recorded correctly. Others have suggested that the stone was nothing more than a hoax or prank.

Roosevelt Buys Stock

The exciting possibility that the Treasure Pit might indeed conceal a treasure worth millions of dollars inspired many others to tackle the problem of the booby-trapped pit. In 1909 an American adventurer and engineer named Henry Bowdoin took over the task of excavating the flooded shaft. He was certain that he could conquer the water traps using modern equip-

U.S. president Franklin D. Roosevelt, pictured here as a young man, was part of a digging crew on Oak Island in 1909.

ment and divers. He formed the Old Gold Salvage and Wrecking Company and sold shares at a dollar apiece. He told investors that there was sure to be treasure worth $10 million in the pit. "With modern methods and machinery the recovery of the treasure is easy, ridiculously easy,"[5] he boasted. With enthusiasm and determination, Bowdoin and his associates purchased the necessary equipment and sailed to Oak Island. They set up camp and named their headquarters after Captain Kidd. They set to work immediately.

One of Bowdoin's original investors was a 27-year-old law clerk named Franklin Delano Roosevelt. As a boy, Roosevelt had spent time at his mother's summer home on Campobello Island in southwest New Brunswick, Canada. He knew about the legendary treasure hunts on nearby Oak Island. In the summer of 1909 he and some of his friends from work took time off to labor with Bowdoin's crew. That summer the men tried to locate the entrance of the flood tunnels at Smith's Cove, but found nothing. Then Bowdoin hired a professional diver. Wearing a large brass deep-sea helmet and a rubber suit, the diver was lowered down into the pit. After returning to the surface, he reported no treasure but said that the wooden beams used long ago to make the pit stable and safe were now crooked and out of alignment, making thorough exploration too difficult.

So Bowdoin ordered several large dynamite

Old Viking Colony

There is scientific proof that the Vikings explored the North American coast before Christopher Columbus's New World landing in the year 1492. Some believe the Treasure Pit is nothing more than remains of a Viking colony.

blasts inside the pit. Afterwards, a steam-powered bucket was used to scoop up smashed timbers, gravel, sand, clay and broken cement. After two frustrating and expensive years without success, Bowdoin gave up trying to recover the mysterious contents of the pit. Disgusted and disappointed, he said in an article published in *Collier's* magazine, "My experience proved to me that there is not and never was a buried treasure on Oak Island. The mystery is solved."[6]

After that first summer, Roosevelt returned to New York and the Wall Street legal firm where he worked. He would later become the 32nd president of the United States. Even as president, Roosevelt still had an interest in the continuing quest for the mysterious treasure. He occasionally received letters from later Oak Island treasure hunters, including Gilbert Hedden and Edwin Hamilton. He replied to their letters. He wished the men success in their search and asked to be updated on their progress.

Disaster Strikes!

Bowdoin's failure certainly did not discourage other treasure hunters. People continued to buy land on Oak Island and to purchase the necessary treasure trove licenses. The licenses gave them legal rights to excavate. Even movie stars Errol Flynn and John Wayne took an interest in recovering the legendary cache. New York multimillionaire Vincent Astor and Antarctic explorer Admiral Richard Byrd were also fascinated by the unsolved mystery. Others who asked about the possibility of restarting the search were men with professional backgrounds in mining or petroleum engineering. There were even those who claimed to be psychics, certain they could locate the treasure through supernatural visions. In 1937 one man insisted he could find the lost gold with his mineral ray wave machine. Another inventor claimed that when he flew over Oak Island in an airplane with his new "treasure smelling machine," the gadget "smashed itself to bits when it smelled the incredible hoard of gold in the depths of the island."[7]

However, no one seemed able to recover the mysterious treasure. People began to say that whatever pirate booty may have once been hoarded in the pit had long been discovered and that there was nothing left to find. Then in the 1950s a man named

Bob Restall moved his wife and children to Oak Island from Ontario, Canada, and resumed the search. The family lived in a one-room shack with no indoor plumbing or electricity. Restall's wife cooked meals using a small propane stove. The home had no phone or running water. Restall used his life's savings to buy the necessary excavation equipment. He

This illustration documents some of the discoveries made through the years in the Treasure Pit.

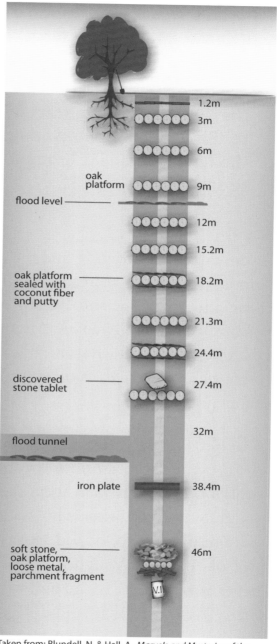

1.2m
3m
6m
oak platform — 9m
flood level —
12m
15.2m
oak platform sealed with coconut fiber and putty — 18.2m
21.3m
24.4m
discovered stone tablet — 27.4m
32m
flood tunnel
iron plate — 38.4m
soft stone, oak platform, loose metal, parchment fragment — 46m

Taken from: Blundell, N. & Hall, A., *Marvels and Mysteries of the Unexplained*, 1989, St. Michael.

even talked his friends and others into donating funds and buying shares in the treasure's recovery. Year after year, he and his son worked in the pit without success. Then in August 1965 the deep shaft flooded again. Restall, his son, and two other men were drowned. No one knows exactly what happened.

Vengeful Ghosts of Oak Island

At the time superstitious people said the tragic deaths of the four men were not accidental. They suggested that ghosts who were seeking revenge were responsible. One old Nova Scotia man, a relative of Anthony Vaughn, told people that he had never been to Oak Island and would not ever go either. "Weird as it may sound, I've seen people there, but not solid people," he said. "Ghosts. I've seen them from my property from when I was a boy up until now. They're ghosts, just wandering around, waiting for something . . . or somebody."[8]

Other spooky legends about Oak Island keep some curious visitors away from the Treasure Pit. There is one long-told tale about a black dog—a dog as big as a colt—with red, fiery eyes that has been seen prowling on the north side of the island. Others say that the large crows and blackbirds on the island are really the spirits of dead treasure seekers keeping an eye on current excavations. Others have heard strange noises, particularly on foggy

Many legends exist about Oak Island, including one about the crows on the island being the spirits of dead treasure hunters.

nights. Restall's widow, Mildred, once admitted that she had experienced many eerie moments while living on Oak Island. Even the current owner of the Treasure Pit, Dan Blankenship, has mentioned hearing strange rumblings beneath the island. Were the noises caused by old shafts and tunnels caving in? Maybe . . . or maybe not.

Chapter 4

The Quest Continues

Over the years, treasure hunters, adventurers, and **archeologists** have continued to come to Oak Island, despite the spooky ghost stories. There is even a creepy old legend that predicts the secret of the pit will not be revealed until all the island's oak trees have died and seven lives have been lost. So far, six men have died trying to recover the treasure. Nevertheless, several fearless people have actually bought property on the island and have lived there full-time. One of them is the current owner, Dan Blankenship, a building contractor. In 1965 he read an article about Oak Island's Treasure Pit in the *Reader's Digest* magazine and decided it was his turn to try to solve the mystery.

Over the years, Blankenship purchased most of the land on Oak Island, determined to find the treasure. He teamed up with Montreal, Canada, millionaire David Tobias. Tobias has spent more than $750,000 to try to recover the mysterious contents of the pit. Blankenship also has spent much time exploring the shoreline near Smith's Cove. There he found huge amounts of coconut fibers buried beneath the beach. His efforts produced more interesting discoveries too, including a very old pair of leather shoes and some antique iron scissors. Experts at the Smithsonian Institution in Washington, D.C., have identified them as the sort once made by Spanish craftsmen in Mexico prior to the 1600s.

Spanish Treasure?

These new discoveries have stirred up Blankenship's imagination and those of treasure seekers around the world. People began to wonder if the pit had been constructed to hide a huge Spanish treasure. Had a Spanish **galleon** loaded with gold

It is thought that treasure on Oak Island could have come from a Spanish galleon that was overtaken by pirates or crashed on the island due to bad weather.

and jewels from Central or South America been forced off course on its return voyage to Spain? For more than two hundred years after Columbus's first voyage to the Americas, Spain plundered the great wealth of the New World. They removed billions of dollars' worth of ore from mines in Mexico and South America, too. They shipped huge amounts of gold, silver, pearls and emeralds upon cargo vessels bound for Europe. To protect the treasure-laden ships from being captured by pirates or attacked by their French and British enemies, the Spanish often organized shipping convoys, where large numbers

of ships sailed together. These Europe-bound convoys routinely sailed within a few hundred miles of Mahone Bay.

Could a violent storm have blown one of the heavy ships into the bay? If so, the ship could have been badly damaged when the crew stopped at Oak Island for repairs. The Spanish captain may have overseen the burying of the treasure chests in a booby-trapped cavern while his crew repaired the ship. He could have designed a system that would have allowed him to dig up the cargo later without springing the booby traps. Perhaps the Spaniards planned to return later for their rich cargo but perished at sea before doing so. According to old Spanish records, many ships loaded with gold and silver from the New World were thought to be lost at sea. They were either sunk by violent storms or captured by murderous buccaneers. The fate of many of these vessels is still unknown to this day.

Borehole 10-X

Excited by the possibility of discovering Spanish treasure, Blankenship and the Triton Salvage Company sunk a borehole, or a deep well, called 10-X about 180 feet (54.86m) northeast of the original Treasure Pit in 1971. It was the deepest hole ever drilled on the island. Using modern mining methods, Triton workers took core samples. These included pieces of china, brass, and parts of a chain made sometime before the year 1750. More samples

Over the years divers have attempted to explore the waters around Oak Island hoping to discover secret passages or hidden treasure.

produced bits of concrete and rust. This meant that some manmade iron object was in the pit. Efforts to pump the seawater out of the pit were unsuccessful, so Blankenship decided to send an underwater camera down into the watery cavern below.

Lack of Oak Trees on Oak Island

A blight killed most of the oak trees on Oak Island in the 1950s and 1960s. However, today new saplings are growing once again.

At 210 feet (64m), the camera revealed a human hand, cut off at the wrist, floating in the cloudy water. The men were amazed! More photo images revealed three wooden chests on the bottom of the cavern. Could these contain long-lost treasure, they wondered? Suddenly, the image of a human body filled the monitor screen. It was slumped against a wall in the underwater chamber and still had flesh and hair intact. The men wondered if their drill had been responsible for severing the hand from the corpse. Excited by these latest discoveries, Blankenship decided to send professional divers into the watery depths to explore further. Blankenship made several dives himself. Unfortunately, the underwater lights were not strong enough to see through the murky waters. The divers, who were tied to safety cables because of the dangerous currents, were limited in how much they could move about.

Then in 1976 Blankenship again took the plunge into Borehole 10-X. He had reached a depth of 145 feet (44.19m) when he heard a deep rumbling noise and felt bits and pieces of items falling around him. He used the headset telephone he wore to call for help. Triton pulled Blankenship to safety. Seconds later, the pit collapsed.

In the meantime, the underwater photos of the human hand and corpse had been sent to others to view. The pictures caused a lot of disagreement. Most people felt the photos taken from the video camera recording system were blurry and difficult to see. A scientist who asked to examine the photograph of the corpse said that the image seemed to indicate a human body that had an obvious jaw and mouth. However, skeptics, or people who questioned the story, pointed out the small chance of a body surviving in one piece after so many years.

Discovery of Sunken Treasure

In 1985 Mel Fisher discovered sunken cargo from the Spanish galleon *Atocha* off the coast of Florida. The overwhelming treasure was valued at more than $450 million.

Then a **pathologist** confirmed that a human body could be preserved underwater over a long period of time if there was a high enough salt content in the water and little air to cause decay. And so, the debate continues.

Myth or Reality?

Many people still wonder if there really is Spanish treasure or pirate loot waiting to be discovered at the bottom of Oak Island's Treasure Pit. Skeptics say no. They insist the pit is nothing more than a natural sinkhole. Others suggest it is an old British ammunition dump dating back to before the French and Indian War of 1754. Some say there is nothing on the island except the settlement remains of the native Micmac people, who once lived there before the European settlers arrived.

And yet there are those who are still hopeful that treasure will be found on Oak Island. Inspired by the thrilling recovery of sunken Spanish gold off the Florida coast, many think the Oak Island treasure should continue to be explored. Some scholars are interested in exploring the site for archaeological purposes. There are even those who want the challenge of outwitting the unknown engineer responsible for the construction of the complicated pit. But Blankenship and his business partner David Tobias, both now elderly and long since retired, have given up the quest. In 2003 they put up their share of Oak Island for sale for $7 million. "If we

Journalist D'Arcy O'Connor, left, has written several pieces on Oak Island. He, along with many others, continues to be fascinated with the mystery that is Oak Island.

factored the buried treasure into the price, we'd be asking for $50 million,"[9] Blankenship said.

The Oak Island Tourism Society has shown an interest in buying the land. It hopes to prevent a developer from building mansions all over the island. The tourism society would like to build a museum with an interpretation center and offer guided tours, making Oak Island a protected heritage site. So far, the organization has not been able to raise enough funds. The lack of money also holds back interested individuals who have new theories about how to successfully excavate the Treasure Pit.

There are those who say treasure hunters eventually will stop pursuing the Oak Island treasure. However, for more than two centuries the pit and its mysterious contents have intrigued the curious and tempted those with a lust for gold. Until the secret is revealed once and for all, the quest will no doubt continue.

Notes

Chapter 1: Buried Treasure

1. Quoted in D'Arcy O'Connor, *The Secret Treasure of Oak Island*. Guilford, CT: Lyons, 2004, p. 18.

Chapter 2: Who Built the Treasure Pit?

2. Quoted in Mike Groushko, *Treasure! Lost, Found & Undiscovered*. Philadelphia: Courage, 1990, p. 20.
3. Quoted in O'Connor, *The Secret Treasure of Oak Island,* p. 245.

Chapter 3: Disappointments and Disasters

4. Quoted in O'Connor, *The Secret Treasure of Oak Island*, p. 12.
5. Quoted in O'Connor, *The Secret Treasure of Oak Island*, p. 67.
6. Quoted in O'Connor, *The Secret Treasure of Oak Island*, p. 70.
7. Quoted in O'Connor, *The Secret Treasure of Oak Island*, p. 132.
8. Quoted in O'Connor, *The Secret Treasure of Oak Island*, p. 159.

Chapter 4: The Quest Continues

9. Quoted in Edward Horton, "Money Pit for Sale." *Fortean Times,* August 2003, p. 30–31.

Glossary

archaeologist: One who studies prehistoric people and their culture.

auger: A drill bit.

booby trap: A device such as a land mine or other trap designed to be triggered when it is touched or disturbed.

blight: A devastating plant disease.

boatswain: A petty officer in charge of the deck crew on a merchant ship.

cache: A place to hide valuables, or the hidden objects themselves.

cofferdams: Large watertight chambers used for construction underwater.

core: A cylinder-shaped sample taken from the ground for research and exploration purposes.

epaulette: A shoulder ornament on a military uniform.

excavate: To dig up.

galleon: A large Spanish commercial sailing ship.

glyphs: Pictographs or other symbolic characters.

inscription: Words engraved or carved into something.

pathologist: A doctor who studies the effects of disease.

plunder: To steal by force; something taken by force.

privateer: A member of a ship's crew authorized by a government to attack enemy vessels.

For Further Exploration

Books

D'Arcy O'Connor, *The Secret Treasure of Oak Island*. Guilford, CT: Lyons, 2004. A detailed report of the amazing true story of the centuries-old treasure riddle of Nova Scotia's notorious Treasure Pit.

J.J. Pritchard, *The Secret Treasures of Oak Island*. Halifax, Nova Scotia: Formac, 2002. An adventure novel in which siblings Joe and Emma spend the summer visiting Nova Scotia and their Uncle Jake, who disappears suddenly while excavating the Treasure Pit.

Alpheus Hyatt Verrill, *They Found Gold! The Story of Successful Treasure Hunts*. Glorieta, NM: Rio Grande, 1972. This book relates the accounts of treasure hunts around the world, including the mysterious Treasure Pit, the hidden treasure of Cocos Island, and the lost mine of Tisingal.

Websites

Historic Mysteries (http://historicmysteries.com/events/the-oak-island-money-pit). This community-based website is devoted to historical mysteries of all sorts, including the elusive Oak Island Treasure Pit, the missing Ark of the Covenant, and the disappearance of Amelia Earhart.

The Museum of Unnatural Mystery (www .unmuseum.org/oakisl.htm). An intriguing website for those interested in learning more about the mystery pit of Oak Island and other fascinating historical sites and unexplained artifacts.

Oak Island Treasure (www.oakislandtreasure .co.uk). This website describes the expeditions and names the people who have searched for buried treasure on the island. Includes photos of Oak Island and the famed Treasure Pit.

Index

Picture Credits

About the Author

Shirley Raye Redmond is the author of several nonfiction books for children, including *The Jersey Devil, Pigeon Hero!* and *Tentacles! Tales of the Giant Squid*. Redmond lives in New Mexico.